From M

From My Heart & Mind

Poems by Neil R Barker

From My Heart and Mind

Copyright © 2018 Neil R Barker

All Rights Reserved

ISBN-13:
978-1985704558
ISBN-10:
1985704552

From My Heart and Mind

From My Heart and Mind

CONTENTS

Dedication
 i

For Angie
 1

When I am feeling my worst
 2

My Best Friend
 3

Hi
 4

Music a big part
 5

I sat and watched the moon
 6

I want to dance with you
 7

Thoughts turn to love
 8

Valentine's Day
 9

From My Heart and Mind

A poem for the holidays
	10

What do I want for Christmas
	11

Until the beach no longer touches the sea
	12

I met someone
	13

I recall a moonlit night
	14

Actually smiling
	15

keeps asking
	16

Bucket list
	17

Dream ride
	18

I love you very much
	19

Darkness attacks
	20

From My Heart and Mind

Hurt in a dream
  21

Hopes, Fears and dreams
  22

Fear cast
  23

Bad dreams and nightmares
  24

Night full of dread
  25

Goodbye Dude (Dude was my Dachshund)
  26

She awaits her love so true
  27

Sitting by the campfire light
  28

To Valhalla
  29

Set sail with the morning tide
  30

One more angel
  31

From My Heart and Mind

A week and a day
    32

Gargoyle
    33

The shepherd
    34

Knight for her love
    35

Aquarium
    36

Strength is what I ask for
    37

Insomnia
    38

Darkness attacks where
    39

You never understood the danger
    40

Beware, something wicked this way comes
    41

Whispers in the rain
    42

From My Heart and Mind

Look out across the ruins
    43

Haunted Woods story begins
    44

Hard to get to know someone
    45

Something about her
    46

Reason for forever
    47

Beauty is in the eye of the beholder
    48

Missing you today
    49

Just missing the girl that I adore
    50

When the one you love
    51

Is love something real
    52

I wish that I could hold you
    53

From My Heart and Mind

Saw your photo
    54

Her blue eyes sparkled
    55

I hate waiting
    56

I tried to write a song
    57

The song I wrote for you
    58

Where are you tonight
    59

How long would you miss me
    60

How many hours
    61

Went shopping but didn't spend a dime
    62

Early summer rain
    63

Walking in the rain for years
    64

From My Heart and Mind

Sun is setting
   65

Not hardly
   66

Paint on a smile
   67

Life is no circus for a sad clown
   68

End of debate
   69

Do you think of me and smile
   70

Dreams will have to do
   71

Give and take
   72

Rode away
   73

Standing in the rain
   74

A memory from the future
   75

From My Heart and Mind

My mind is wandering today
    76

Joy abounds
    77

Is there something more that I can say
    78

I fell in love with you
    79

Walking through the park
    80

Peace inside
    81

Remember me
    82

The one true love of my life
    83

Friendship to love
    84

Size and shape of love
    85

I wanted to tell you how much I care
    86

From My Heart and Mind

I'd send a poem to your printer
    87

If I asked to kiss thee
    88

If I told you that I love you
    89

Second to none
    90

Slow walk in the rain
    91

Smile, no choice
    92

Standing at the rail
    93

The truth I hold within
    94

Those eyes
    95

What is it that makes us fall in love
    96

When I see you, my heart skips a beat
    97

From My Heart and Mind

Would you sit
    98

Never intend to
    99

Hung a dream catcher above my bed
    100

Good times light our way
    101

Broken block
    102

Mom died
    103

Never stood a chance
    104

Dragon
    105

When life goes astray
    106

I love you , my sweet
    107

Kiss my muse
    108

From My Heart and Mind

Last kiss
	109

Wonderfully in love with you
	110

About the author
	II

From My Heart and Mind

DEDICATION PAGE

I'm dedicating this book to Angie Schuler.

My best friend, my confidante, my rock.

Without her in my life, this collection of poems that I have written wouldn't have been possible.

Life as I know it, is a direct result of

her friendship, advice, and support.

In honor of the most amazing and important lady in my life,

Angie, I love you very much and this is for you!

From My Heart and Mind

From My Heart and Mind

I had always hoped we could have coffee and talk.

Now I don't see that happening with you going on this walk.

To know you better was my only thought.

No more than you would willingly offer had I sought.

You have been my friend and always will be, for so long as you'll have me.

My heart breaks with knowing that your smile I'll never again see.

You must do as you must... this I understand.

But I doubt to ever again know a lady so grand.

Please remember me fondly is the best I can ask for in the end.

Because I dearly love you, my friend.

From My Heart and Mind

When I am feeling my worst,

My heart and mind look to you first.

When there's nowhere to turn for comfort during a downhill slide.

I would crawl for miles to get to your side.

You are the love of my life, my world, my muse, my everything.

Life without you in it, just isn't worth living.

Perfect? No, I would never accuse you of that.

Amazing and wonderful and as majestic as a cat .

To kiss your lips and hold you in my arms,

Would be to know an angel's charms.

You make a house into a home.

Without you I'm little more than a garden gnome.

Come hold my hand and walk with me.

I would give my all to have more time with thee.

You could wrap me around your fingers since you already hold my heart.

You mean everything to me and that's just the start.

Angie, I love you!

And this you know is true.

From My Heart and Mind

Sometimes things happen that we never intend.

And so, I fell in love with you, my best friend.

You are beyond beautiful in my eyes.

You will always be the rainbow in my skies.

You were there when I went through my hardest, darkest times.

In spirit you were there with me, as certainly as a bell chimes.

You talked with me across the miles.

The sound of your voice brought me smiles.

When I was about to lose control.

You brought sunshine to my soul.

Your words are always what I need to hear.

Once in a while the words I want, from the one I hold most dear.

A girlfriend, a lover I try to find.

My problem, is that you are always on my mind.

My heart belongs to you and always will.

Because you ask me to, I search still.

But I have found the love of my life, my soul mate, you see.

I am in love with the most wonderful woman, my best friend, Angie.

From My Heart and Mind

Hi, Allow me to introduce myself. I am a dreamer.

A dreamer believes and fights for what they want, even

when their foundation is no stronger than a streamer.

A dreamer believes in true love, romance, winning and success, no matter what

They strive for the best life's got.

Unfortunately, dreamers , in the end, often wind up alone.

They get so focused on their rainbows ends, they lose the ones that would call them their own.

I like to think that there is a little bit of dreamer in everyone.

Here's a piece of wisdom I'd like to pass along before I'm done.

The key to happiness it would appear is "everything in moderation"

I'm a dreamer and happiness is just a fleeting temptation.

True dreamers are often misunderstood you see.

They are simply put, rainbow chasers of the nth degree.

Beyond shadow, beyond light.

Ever searching for a truth that's worth the fight.

From My Heart and Mind

Music a big and important part of my life.

It was there during good times and saw me through strife.

Alone or with friends,

Music played beyond modern trends.

Certain songs bring to mind

Memories and times that were not always kind.

Yet I treasure them, every one.

They are part of who I have become.

The most cherished and dear to my heart,

Are the ones that remind me of my life when you were a part.

From My Heart and Mind

I sat and watched the moon rise above the horizon on a crisp fall night.
Romance filled the air, but alone was I in the moonlight.
My heart began to sing a song and I saw pictures of you in my mind.
Your sparkling eyes, filled with kindness and a love I hope to find.
Tell me, how do I reach your heart?
What would it take to give "us" a start?
Should I grab my phone and give you a call?
You know that I love you most of all.
Are you alone beneath this same autumn moon?
Is my name sung in your hearts tune?
On a night like this, do you have thoughts about me?
I pray that someday, someway, a loving couple we'll be.
Tell me, how do I reach your heart?
What would it take to give "us" a start?
Should I grab my phone and give you a call?
You know that I love you most of all.
(music break)
Tell me, how do I reach your heart?
What would it take to give "us" a start?
Should I grab my phone and give you a call?
You know that I love you most of all.
(*PHONE RINGS*)
(*fading out*) Hi, I was just thinking about you. How are you doing?

From My Heart and Mind

From My Heart and Mind

I want to dance with you.

We'll dance the whole night through.

When something slow, the dj plays,

I'll hold you close and we will sway.

I want to dance with you.

We'll rest for a song or two.

Babe, will you dance with me?

I love you, can't you see?

I want to dance with you.

They give last call at two.

Please be my partner my whole life through.

Babe, I'm so in love with you.

I want to dance with you.

I want to dance with you!

From My Heart and Mind

Valentine's Day, when everyone's thoughts turn to love.

With hearts, gifts and chocolates and cupid's arrows from above.

The person most special to you gets asked "will you be mine?"

An answer of "yes", makes you feel positively divine.

If you are together with this one, hugs and kisses are in order.

But if miles separate you, hopes and dreams you grasp like a hoarder.

Tell them and let them know how much you care.

This Valentine's Day, when love is in the air.

Missing someone and being alone.

Praying for a text or to hear their voice on the phone.

A substitute for hugs and kisses, your heart flutters like a dove.

On Valentine's Day, when everyone's thoughts turn to love.

From My Heart and Mind

I wanted to write you a poem for Valentine's Day

But my emotions kept getting in the way.

It seems Cupid's arrows never miss

He's been using my heart for target practice.

My heart must look like a pin cushion judging how I feel

His darts of love, my fate did seal.

He's mean, but I'm not going to complain,

Even though I know this love is in vain.

He shot my heart now overflowing with love for you

Yet, he didn't loose a single one to return those feelings too.

Valentine's Day we recognize love

And celebrate being struck by those arrows from above.

But it's not the only day that we recognize the one closest to our hearts

From My Heart and Mind

You would still be that one every day, even without his darts

I will adore you from afar until I give up the ghost.

When we are together we are friends, first and foremost.

You need never wonder if anyone cares

Be it major or minor, I'll always be there

I will stand beside you through thick and thin

It doesn't matter what, where or when.

And when February rolls round you needn't ask " Will you be mine?"

Because I forever will be your Valentine!

From My Heart and Mind

A poem for the holidays

The words came out sideways.

It didn't rhyme or flow

So in the trash it had go.

I couldn't figure what was wrong

It was like there was no melody to a song.

It was simply no use

Trying to create without my muse.

Where are you tonight?

I'm so lost without your guiding light.

When I see you again I'll be too much in awe to say.

I need you, I want you, I love you more every day.

I hope life doesn't keep us apart.

If it does, surely I will die of a broken heart.

I have looked everywhere on earth for the one I adore.

I guess next, I'll climb the stairs that lead to heavens' door.

Or I can stay and wait here

Alone with the darkness and fear.

From My Heart and Mind

What do I want for Christmas?

I want to spend it with you.

We'll spend the day together just we two.

We'll look into each other's eyes until we start laughing like a couple of fools.

This is our day together, there are no rules.

We'll walk hand in hand to the mistletoe and stop for a kiss or two.

You see, my only wish for Christmas is you.

Coffee and doughnuts for breakfast will do.

It matters not to me, as long as I am with you.

Songs of the season play.

We'll sing along in our odd way.

I love you more and deeper than you can imagine.

I would happily spend eternity with you and replay this day again and again.

Just to make certain there's no doubt in your mind.

From the bottom of my heart " I Love You " and will until far beyond the end of time.

From My Heart and Mind

How long will I love thee?

Until the beach no longer touch the sea.

Would you think of me less or more,

If you understood that it is you I truly adore?

I wish I were your heart's desire.

Just a thought of you sets my heart on fire.

Am I the one you dream about?

You are the one I don't want to live without.

Do you think of me fondly or am I just a lump of coal?

I will always love you with all my heart, mind, body and soul.

I can't help but wonder if you have any feelings for me.

I hope you now know at least, how much I love thee.

From My Heart and Mind

I met someone a short while ago.
Someone that touched me deeper than they know.
A beautiful person both outside and in.
Just knowing her makes my life a win.
Does she have an inkling of how much I care?
Do I tell her in earnest? No, I do not dare.
I think she is beautiful, funny and smart.
When she smiles it warms my heart.
The cute way she crinkles her nose,
makes me wonder if she knows.
That something so simple makes my spirits soar.
I imagine that a hug would touch my very core.
A kiss beneath the mistletoe, would be more intoxicating than wine.
I can imagine no other reason why her lips would ever touch mine.
If I could find the nerve some day,
to her this is what I would say.
"I always thought of Romeo as an idiot, and a fool too,
But now he makes perfect sense, if his Juliet were half as wonderful as you."

From My Heart and Mind

I recall a moonlit night like tonight.

and being too shy to tell you the things I might.

how beautiful I knew you to be.

shyly hoping that in my eyes you would see.

That I loved you with my heart, body and soul.

Just to kiss your lips, seemed like too lofty a goal.

To touch your hand which was mere inches away.

My heart longs to be so near to you today.

My feelings have not faded over the years.

I can feel the sting tonight as my eyes fill with tears.

Now a lonely man stands where a shy youth once stood.

In the moon light I stand alone and wonder if today I could.

Tell you of the feelings I hold still deep within.

Or would I be silent, yet again?

If you should read this, please believe these words are true.

Throughout eternity, I will always love you!

From My Heart and Mind

It must be a dream, I can't be awake.

I was actually smiling for goodness sakes.

I smiled and you smiled, what a wonderful life.

For a little while my mind felt no strife.

Is it you? Is it me? Is it us? Is there an us?

That would explain my heart raising such a fuss.

Your eyes, your lips, the touch of your hand,.

Gets my mind whirling like the blades of a fan.

I don't know where or when,

But I'm looking forward to seeing you again!

From My Heart and Mind

My status update keeps asking what's on my mind.

If I answered honestly no one would believe an answer of that kind.

I have a sense of humor that's here to stay.

It's a bit warped some would say.

I laugh at myself because my mind is a jumbled mess.

There's just one thing that stays on my mind, I must confess.

Her name, I will not share.

I always hope, that she knows and how much I care.

Beauty is in the heart and can be seen with the mind's eye.

In a gray existence she is the full color rainbow in the sky.

She's beautiful inside and out.

Others would concur, I have no doubt.

From My Heart and Mind

I look forward to waking up in the morning.

Each new day offers the chance for a glimpse of her without warning.

I would gladly look upon her every day.

She's amazing to me, I don't know what else to say.

A short, familiar phrase is all "what's on my mind" boils down to.

And that is, "I Love You!"

From My Heart and Mind

What does a bucket list contain?

things to do and need not explain.

hearts desires and wonders to see,

what to do before our souls are set free.

Places to go and people to meet.

before the grim reaper we each shall greet.

Things to taste and sounds to hear.

Fears to face down and our consciences to clear.

Things of this world we don't want to miss.

At the top for me... your lips to kiss!

From My Heart and Mind

Do you know how much I'd love to kiss your lips?

When you walk away do you know how my heart rips?

Do you know how wonderful it would be to hold your hand?

My love for you is not written in sand.

What secret does my heart know?

How a simple thought of you makes it glow.

How exactly you feel, I do not know.

Away from you, how my tears flow.

Do you care the same way I do?

Do you know that the moon brings me thoughts of you?

How fantastic would it be to stand at your side?

My minds best guess I know only from a dream ride.

From My Heart and Mind

The passing of my mother was the darkest moment of my life so far.

At that moment my world crashed down around me and everything seemed bizarre.

My heart and mind reached out for the one I adore.

Then I went into a survivors mode, I'm sure.

I detached from my emotions and followed where logic led.

I proceeded to pack and make the arrangements as they came into my head.

The phone rang and I heard the voice of the one I love.

The sound of her voice, for me, was a gift from God above.

She'll never understand what she means to my life.

My muse, my comfort, my heart's desire, my soul's wife.

Because I listened to her, I got to spend,

From My Heart and Mind

precious time with my mom near the end.

I've reconnected with my family.

The divorce I desired has become a reality.

I accept that my best friend is the most she wishes to be.

Because, life without her would be meaningless and empty.

No joy, no sunshine, no love, no reason to live.

My life would be as pointless as pouring water through a sieve.

"I love you very much, so you be careful." a few days later she said to me.

My love, I am yours, to have and to hold for all eternity.

From My Heart and Mind

The darkness approached with the intent of over taking me.

The bright light inside of me it couldn't see.

All it saw, as did the world, was the sorrow I showed.

Blinded by it's thirst for the blood, in my veins, that flowed.

It rushed forward, full attack, planning on taking body and soul.

It never suspected I'd face it and stop it from reaching its goal.

Like a flash of light, brighter than lightening, and the darkness screamed.

As my thoughts of you filled me with love and my eyes beamed.

The darkness never stood a chance, and it didn't have a clue.

Defeated before it started, because of how much I am in love with you!

From My Heart and Mind

I remember the dream as if it were last night.

Dressed in battle armor, and in one major fight.

The group moving forward in a main tunnel going down.

Good versus evil a war underground.

The enemy would retreat, then turn and fight.

Many casualties fell on both sides that night.

During one such skirmish a secondary attack came.

From a side tunnel my life they tried to claim.

A bite attack is what it tried.

My armor held, and that enemy died.

I remember not after that point of the dream.

But I had a souvenir it would seem.

I found marks in the shape of that monster's bite.

And painful ribs which are still sore to the touch to this very night!

From My Heart and Mind

Hopes, fears, and dreams

They are a part of each of us it seems.

They guide us, protect us and drive us on.

Some stay with us forever, others are fleeting and gone.

Sometimes from time we try to hide.

That's silly really, because they come from inside.

We hope for something better, and fear that which is unknown.

But we should dream big, because that is the only one we own.

Hope requires faith beyond what is inside.

Fear holds us back and makes us set our goals aside.

Dreams are what life is all about!

Without them, we'd all be down and out.

From My Heart and Mind

Fear cast a shadow that made me groan.

The fear of being forever alone.

I had been blinded over time.

Isolated without reason or rhyme.

Where love once sang proud and strong,

I awoke to hear a most twisted song.

What once masqueraded as love for me,

Believed me broken and unable to leave.

After facing the physical, mental and emotional abuse.

I broke the self made chains that kept me from breaking loose.

I made a vow with myself as I walked out the door...

I will be a prisoner no more!

From My Heart and Mind

Bad dreams and nightmares.

I keep them to myself because no one cares.

Pick myself up in spite of the lack of sleep.

No one wants to get too close or in too deep.

I walk alone through the surging crowd.

Screaming a silent scream out loud.

Attention, none do I gather, not so much as an eyelash batter.

I walk as if invisible because I do not matter.

I could fall off the planet and no one would notice it seems.

No one, nothing, except perhaps the nightmares and bad dreams.

From My Heart and Mind

I remember a night full of dread.

I felt someone sit upon the edge of my bed.

I awoke and was chilled to the bone.

I was in my bedroom all alone.

I recall the dark things as well as the light.

Both gave a younger me such a fright.

Now wiser and much older for sure.

I look back fondly at the haunted house near Jersey Shore.

Spirits cross my path to this very day.

I do what I can to help them find their way.

The dark ones try me and test my faith and will.

But today they find a fighter unwavering and still.

A new bout has started with shadows and voice.

Drive them away now is the smarter choice.

Before they grow strong and add to their number.

Then at night I can have peaceful, restful, uninterrupted slumber.

From My Heart and Mind

A tear rolled down my heart today.

Thoughts of you here, but you have gone away.

I can still see the love in your eyes.

And remember the heartbreak of saying our goodbyes.

I still love you and did even when you were in a bad mood.

It's crazy how much I miss you...Dude.

RIP August 1, 1999 - September 27, 2015

Note: Dude was a beloved Dachshund, his name was Dusty

but we called him Dude.

From My Heart and Mind

Standing on the hillside looking out across the bay.

In a field of wildflowers on a sunny summer's day.

Holding in her hand a picnic lunch for two.

She awaits her love so true.

Her eyes stare at the pathway and begins to daydream.

How wonderful their future together seems.

The day's shadows grow long and still she waits.

She must leave soon to be safe within the hamlet's gates.

How deep her love, to so yearn.

For a love, which will never return.

From My Heart and Mind

Sitting by the campfire light.

I look up at a star filled summer's night.

A wish for you I asked upon the first star I saw.

Pictures of you even here does my mind draw.

Good health, good fortune and love be yours.

Tonight and forever I hope happiness endures.

For you deserve nothing less than the finest and best.

May sweet dreams always accompany your rest.

So from here beside my campfire,

To you, my heart's one desire,

Anything for you never asking why.

I bid thee good life...for tomorrow I die.

From My Heart and Mind

I had a visitor while I slept.

She whispered to me and we wept.

A friend had gone by Valkyrie wings.

No more shall we talk of things.

To battle an unseen foe.

What a courageous way to go.

A coward this cancer that kills from within.

I will always remember and grin.

To Valhalla in the end.

A fitting place for you my friend.

From My Heart and Mind

I leaned upon the rail, wind in my face.

How do I tell them, this is not the place.

A long hard trek to get here.

Further still to go, and worse to come I fear.

I left with a crew of raw young boys.

Let them relax and make some noise.

The ones that survive to make port back home.

Will be strong seasoned veterans, beyond the best in Rome.

So, for today eat, drink and be merry, for tomorrow we die.

We'll set sail with the morning tide.

From My Heart and Mind

I heard a song the other night.

It brought to mind a picture of you in the sunlight.

I could almost smell your perfume on the air.

And hear laughter like we used to share.

That summer, when this song was new,

We sang along, if we only knew.

That was the last summer we would share.

Did you know, or did it come from out of nowhere?

That fall, as the leaves fell so did my tears.

I still miss you after all these years.

I guess heaven needed one more angel that day.

Maybe if I'm real good, we'll get to sing again that way.

From My Heart and Mind

It's been a week and a day.
Since you passed away.
It was your time to leave.
Now is my time to grieve.
Nevermore will I see you smile.
Even when we didn't keep in touch, mom, I loved you all the while.
Right now, I feel like I'm falling apart.
Crying today stems from the love for you in my heart.
A piece of you will live on within me.
And I shall always cherish each memory.
The times we spent together, by design or by chance.
I'll always treasure the night you got out of your wheelchair, so we could once more dance.
From you I learned what a "home" should be.
It's not a house, or a place, but a heart filled with love, for all the world to see.
My heart holds this love inside, and someday, another will understand.
And our dance will be special, and I will hold her hand.
Just like you and dad, forever in love.
Here on earth and now in heaven above.

From My Heart and Mind

The gargoyle kept watch from his tower perch.

For what, I wonder, does his stony eyes search?

Long forgotten are those that laid siege to this keep.

And disturbed the gargoyle's sleep.

Buried beneath time's flowing sands.

Are those that invaded gargoyle protected lands.

From My Heart and Mind

Watching, waiting for the call
the shepherd rescues any and all.
Those that call for him know
He will be there to take them in tow.
In the middle of the night
or in the brightest daylight
He is there waiting for the word to be given
this servant unto heaven.
Watching, waiting as souls pass by
the shepherd oft wonders why.
Why do they stray from the road,
do they forget what they've been told?
How far will they stray,
before they lose their way,
and ask forgiveness from the Lord?
Then the shepherd shall deliver them from the evil hoard.
Back to the path of narrow and straight.
This is the call for which he doth wait.
Watching, waiting, prepared to fight.
The shepherd is a warrior of light.
With a flaming sword of light in hand
he will fight for souls in the darkest land.
A loss loses a soul, but with a victory it can be saved,
 and returned to where the pathway is paved.
So fear not if into the darkness you should fall,
remember the shepherd is watching and
waiting to answer the call.

From My Heart and Mind

From My Heart and Mind

Deep in the darkness, facing certain defeat.

In my mind, her voice touched my heart, and I rose to my feet.

A strength came from somewhere deep within.

This was a battle that I must win.

My sword washed in a bright white light.

The evil split and fled from my very sight.

The love that filled my heart, it can't withstand.

To reach her side, my minds only command.

I'd slay dragons to win her hand and heart.

To disperse hoards to keep her safe, I'll do my part.

The bards will call her my battle muse.

For her, facing any danger I won't refuse.

Guided by the light from heaven above.

I am a knight, because of her love.

From My Heart and Mind

An aquarium, a living relaxation zone.

Enjoyable as a group or when you're alone.

The fun in designing the tank's decor.

Inside and out from cover to floor.

A work of art and one of a kind.

Set a theme of what's on your mind.

Fresh or salt water depends on the fish.

You can have whichever you wish.

Don't be afraid to go all out.

Your well being is what it's about.

From My Heart and Mind

Strength is what I ask for dear lord.

To face each day, to continue forward.

To stand as the man I should be

To make my loved ones proud of me.

Give me the strength to be tender and kind.

And to speak what's on my mind.

I understand strength isn't all about power

Nor just being steadfast during the darkest hour.

It takes great strength to show compassion

When slaughter would seem the correct action.

Give me the strength to use the gifts you've given me.

To make this world a better place to be.

From My Heart and Mind

My mind is whirling here in the dark.

I wish, like my car I could shift it into park.

The alarm goes off in two hours or less.

To work I'll go, what a mess.

My mind is running amok in the night.

Afraid to force focus and see what I might.

The girl my arms long to hold.

A smile, heavenly to behold.

Her painted lips, I would so hungrily taste.

Without her, my life seems such a waste.

So, my thoughts I dump into the void.

And welcome the peaceful slumber, for the time left, to be enjoyed.

Relaxing and clearing my mind of all thought.

Insomnia, I've beat you; battle well fought.

From My Heart and Mind

The darkness attacks where you are most vulnerable.

Guard your heart and home with light undeniable.

Keep your trust and faith in the light.

Your burdens will ease in regards to your plight.

If you lose sight and start to fall.

Reach out for the light, it will respond to your call.

You'll need down time and lots of rest.

Forgive and forget that would be best.

Ask a shepherd to watch over your sleep.

Like one of the flock, your safety will keep.

A shepherds job to rescue and protect.

You may not see them, but you will feel their effect.

May your spirit and soul find peace.

May the light fill and surround you and the darkness cease!

From My Heart and Mind

You never understood the danger.

You just kept pushing my anger.

My voice got louder like a warning bell.

But still you couldn't tell.

Push, shove and ire raised.

You saw for an instant my mind furious and crazed.

Now it seems you're trying again.

To release from me the demon within.

Not to banish it; no that's not your aim.

You want to play with it like some sort of game.

Bent on destruction beyond your wildest dream.

In my nightmares I see its eyes gleam.

It awaits for a weak moment to break free.

You did your worst and wounded me.

Now before I blink or slightly sway.

I'm going to just turn and walk away.

From My Heart and Mind

My mind is clouded by music from the past.
Hoping to regain clear thought but the list of songs is vast.
Even to set a short message down
My thoughts randomness is as funny as a clown.
A headache pounds like drums.
The screaming pitch in my ears would reduce crystal to crumbs.
When rest is not coming sleep will do.
This is just like a when a weird fog falls over you.
Not used to this feeling in the middle of the day.
Need someone to lean on 'til this feeling goes away.
Someone to protect me that I can trust.
That won't take advantage of a tin man covered in rust.
Be they human or be they Fae,
Someone to have my back or lead the way.
No matter what the tally sums.
BEWARE - Something Wicked This Way Comes.

reference: 1962 story by Ray Bradbury....Something wicked this way comes.

From My Heart and Mind

Your heart holds a secret that will cause me pain.

I heard that truth from whispers in the rain.

I believed that together we'd ride life's train.

Until my heart listened to whispers in the rain.

'Tis sad to know my lips, yours will never stain.

My dreams of us have been shattered by whispers in the rain.

Dark clouds keep secrets we'd rather wash down the drain.

But all is told by whispers in the rain.

From My Heart and Mind

I look out across the ruins and wonder what happened here.

How beautiful must this place have been, 'tis hard to hold back a tear.

The statues, the architecture, the beauty hinted at; by what is left behind.

What city or town stood here? none. this is the landscape of my mind.

The decay area gives way to an area of rebirth .

new art , buildings , a reflection of my, self worth.

Instead of rebuilding and clearing the damage away

I keep the reminders like a museum of a twisted day.

The ruins were caused by a broken heart.

Mending , a new age of beauty begins with a fresh start.

From My Heart and Mind

From My Heart and Mind

Walking along the forest trail.
I paused as I thought of the old folk tale.
Within these woods a magic lives.
The story this warning gives.
Don't leave the trail where the green moss grows.
Else feel the sting of arrows from tiny bows.
I wish I remembered the rest of the story.
The moss covers the trail, I think it's time to worry.
Magic is at work within the enchanted woods.
Moss covering the trail can't mean anything good.
I don't normally walk this way.
Just wanted to clear my thoughts today.
Strange, the sounds I hear.
Off in the distance, yet beautiful and clear.
Too long have I listened, my mind starts to scream.
Twilight has fallen and I have awakened inside a bad dream.
I hear my name and look about.
I wonder if I could follow this pathway out.
There, my name again, who's calling me?
Oh, the proper response, hmmm let me see.
Tis I, if friend come and be well met.

From My Heart and Mind

If foe be gone and be no blood let.
I am unarmed and just invited someone unseen to join me on the path.
I perhaps have gone daft.
Well said. I've not heard a proper greeting response in many years.
I am a friend, I've come to calm your fears.
I'll join you on the path in a moment.
Need to be sure word of our meeting is sent.
Onto the path appears an elf.
I know this from the drawing book that was kept on a high shelf.
It was the most treasured possession in the house.
Yet here I stand, quiet as a mouse.

From My Heart and Mind

It's hard to get to know someone, when there is no time to talk.

And nowhere to take a secluded walk.

You have to work from impressions and go off of what you know .

And hope you understood the nuances so.

Life runs by its own rule.

It just seems that to me it is always being cruel.

From My Heart and Mind

There is something about her.

Something that invades my slumber.

She's like warm wonderful dreams.

Can she be as true as she seems?

Smart and beautiful and full of fun.

With eyes that sparkle like diamonds in the sun.

She pulls her hair back and shows a neck that would make a vampire drool.

This lady proves that Romeo was not a fool.

For if Juliet were so fair,

Death is better than life without a woman to whom, none other can compare.

From My Heart and Mind

Trying to find the reason for forever.

I'm thinking that the answer is going to be something clever.

It's a goal that lovers set.

For most, unattainable but yet,

For a precious few, being in love with one another lasts a lifetime and will continue beyond .

So, is forever only about soul mates bond?

Does forever end when we die?

Or is it as seemingly endless as the stars in the sky?

Is forever just something to believe in?

A reason religion uses to scare people away from sin?

For me, just in case forever is true.

Then it's just the start of how long I want to be with you.

From My Heart and Mind

Beauty is in the eye of the beholder.

Do I perceive it differently now that I'm older?

Could I always see the beauty that is within?

Or was I blind to it like so many men?

I don't recall of ever trying for the girl with the prettiest face.

But when I tried, she was always someone that could set my heart a pace.

Never had much luck getting a date with any girl that I asked out.

Today is not different, my feelings are something apparently to be kicked about.

From My Heart and Mind

The one that holds my heart, I'll never ask for a date, for goodness sakes.

To keep her in my life, I'll do whatever it takes.

I am in love with a lady I find to be beautiful outside and in.

Without her in my life, the day would have no reason to begin.

From My Heart and Mind

Missing you today makes me feel sad.

My worst fears don't make me feel so bad.

Knowing you are out there somewhere.

Keeps me watching to see if you are there.

Waiting to see you again weighs heavy on my heart.

It seems like something evil keeps us apart.

When I get to see you I'll know such joy.

I'll feel like a child that just got a new toy.

Until them I'll miss you so.

Please stay then...I won't want you to go.

Without you I am but an empty shell.

Rescue me please from this evil spell.

I long to hold you in my arms so tight.

and to kiss your lips...will be like a deliverance into the light.

This inner darkness will be forever cast away.

From My Heart and Mind

When we are once more together on oh such a blessed day.

I'll whisper I love you softly in your ear.

and I'll cherish you and keep you always near.

Until then my mind is filled with thoughts of you.

And oft I wonder if you likewise miss me too.

From My Heart and Mind

Something seems so wrong.
Friday nights are meant for wine, women and song.
Yet here I am walking alone in the grocery store.
For company, I have store music and faded memories of the girl I adore.
Perhaps I am out of my mind.
Maybe life is just unkind.
Up and down like a roller coaster my emotions go.
How do I tell her that I love her so?
Too far away to touch her hand
Too tired and confused to understand.
Alas, to hold her close and sway slowly to the music of our hearts.
Is this how a sweet dream starts?
If being in love with her is a dream, let me sleep.
This feeling, like the ocean runs deep.
Tonight I'll tell the stars about the one I love.
Perhaps we'll find ourselves together, thanks to some nudging from above.
For now I am wandering the store
Just missing the girl that I adore.

From My Heart and Mind

When the one you are in love with isn't in love with you.
It makes no difference what you say or do.
When you feel that your soul is the perfect mate for theirs.
You try to tell them and show them but they seem not to care.
Your heart is theirs and theirs alone.
Your love is not flighty or windblown.
They are not a whim, a fancy nor an object of lust.
They are the one you'll love long after you've turned to dust.
You'll try hard to move on and find someone else to be with.
But even then your thoughts betray you like a sith.
Holding them is evil and their feelings you abuse.
Because your love belongs eternally to your muse.
You say the words and play the part like an actor on a stage.
Yet inside, all the while, your conscience is screaming with rage.
Because your every dream, wish, desire will never come true.
You are an empty shell, when the one you are in love with, isn't in love with you.

From My Heart and Mind

Is love something real?

If so, is it a forever deal?

If your heart thumps to loves throng,

Why are there so many heartbreak songs?

I once knew a magical feeling I called love.

The magic went away and life went from push to shove.

I tried to restore the magic like rekindling a fire.

But nothing remained as though it had been part of a funeral pyre.

Is there an eternal magic in the world for me?

Is there a love to outlast the sea?

I don't want the hope for love to leave.

So, yes there is...or at least that's what I believe.

From My Heart and Mind

I wish that I could hold you in my arms tonight.

You would feel the love that burns bonfire bright.

A kiss from your lips, what might this simple key unlock?

A lust, a passion, a lover or animal starting with kisses by the flock.

Would this be what is set loose within you?

It certainly would be freed in me too.

From your lips to the nape of your neck my mouth would go.

Not in a single jump, yet too quickly to be considered slow.

Like fire in the wind we'd be swept away.

My wildest dreams wouldn't hold a candle to this day.

Starting out in each other's arms, did you dare dream?

Would lead to a passion hotter than steam.

From My Heart and Mind

I saw your photo and I knew.

There was something special about you.

That smile, those eyes.

I felt an attraction I can't disguise.

I wondered, is this an angel from above,

is this the woman which I'm meant to love?

What do I say to her that will let me see,

If she might feel the same way about me?

My mind says, don't come on too strong.

My heart says, this is where I belong.

My arms say, hold her and all will be revealed.

My lips just smile and say nothing, as if they've been sealed.

Is she the muse I'm to spend my life with?

Or is true love, like the unicorn, just a myth?

From My Heart and Mind

Her blue eyes sparkled as she glanced into mine.

I'd ask her for a kiss, if she would but show a sign.

against my chest, she buried her face,

as we held tightly our embrace.

Too soon came our time to part.

watching her drive away nearly broke my heart.

Maybe I'll see her tomorrow, or perhaps she'll call.

Moving forward is harder than I recall.

From My Heart and Mind

I hate waiting for the phone to ring.

That style of patience is not my thing.

While I await my love to call,

I imagine a portrait of her upon the wall.

It would be like seeing her face every day.

Her beauty would brighten the room in every way.

Does she know how much I love her? Does she care?

The bright center of my existence, this lady fair.

I am so in love with her, just saying, that's all.

So here I sit, just longing for her to call.

From My Heart and Mind

I tried to write a song,

But the words just sounded wrong.

I tried to write a story,

But the plot made me worry.

I tried to write a poetic rhyme,

But it flowed out of time.

My hand only wanted to write a simple phrase that would be eternally true.

No matter what the future holds, I am in love with you!

From My Heart and Mind

I sang the song I wrote for you.

For the first time others heard it too.

Last night I opened my heart so the people could see.

I poured my emotions out, yet stood still as a tree.

My mind had me looking into your eyes.

Everyone knew these words held no lies.

Tears streamed down my face.

By the end I knew you were not in this place.

All who heard knows my heart is yours until the end of time.

But they will never know yours, will never be mine.

From My Heart and Mind

Do you know that I miss you in the glow of candle light?

I can't help but wonder, what you're doing tonight.

This feeling is a daily thing growing stronger with time.

And I miss you with every clock chime.

Though I know I will see you soon,

'Twas a promise between you, me and the moon.

Still I wonder how you're feeling tonight

In your dreams would I be a welcome sight?

My love for you grows stronger with each passing day,

Sometimes it feels like you are walking further away.

You wrapped in my loving arms, much to my delight.

But instead I wonder, where are you tonight?

From My Heart and Mind

How long would you miss me?

A day, a week or throughout eternity?

Absence makes the heart grow fonder or so they say.

But being away from you is such a high price to pay.

My heart would be broken if we were torn apart.

Eternity is where my missing you would start.

I know how strong my love is for you dear.

But your true feelings for me are as yet unclear.

How long to forget me, a year, a month, an hour?

Do you really care?

would you notice if I were not there?

My heartfelt tears could flood a sea.

Answer this question I put to thee.

If being apart we should ever be,

would you miss me?

From My Heart and Mind

How many hours behind the wheel,

Until the touch of your hand I will feel?

How many days must go by,

Before I may gaze into your eyes?

Is it wrong to let slip,

That I long to kiss your lips?

Where is the harm,

In wanting to hold you in my arms?

Nibbling your neck, would that quench your desire,

Or perhaps stoke a passionate fire?

'Tis madness being this far apart.

The waiting to hold you tight and feel the beating of your heart.

Call me soon that I may hear your voice.

My making the drive to see you is the obvious choice.

From My Heart and Mind

I had a dream the other night.

The memory stayed of a wonderful sight.

We went shopping but didn't spend a dime.

Two friends laughing, talking having a nice time.

Went back to my apartment and had a bite to eat.

I tossed together a southwest pizza and we opted for no meat.

Spending time together was the most fun I've had in years.

When you said you had to go it near brought me to tears.

I'd forgotten what it was like having company to enjoy.

I felt like a kid at Christmas opening a new toy.

I pray it was a glimpse of times yet to be.

It means a brighter future is ahead for me.

From My Heart and Mind

Sitting watching an early summer rain.

A shower, bringing a peacefulness to my brain.

In the rain my mind begins to drift.

A memory comes strong and swift.

A lady, the rain, a cigarette in hand.

Her eyes, a smile, my heart soaring above the land.

Talking with this beauty, my friend by choice.

I have always loved hearing her voice.

An amazing woman, that has stolen my heart.

Funny, beautiful, kind and smart.

It's little wonder you can see.

I will love her throughout eternity!

From My Heart and Mind

Walking in the rain, something I've enjoyed for years.

Free relaxation therapy to clear the mind with nature sounds for the ears.

Put the umbrella away and walk with me.

Come enjoy this summer afternoon rain, you'll see.

The clean feel of the rain on my face is good for my psych.

We can even talk if you'd like.

Some say it's romantic, I think it's pure.

But it's just a treatment not a cure.

From My Heart and Mind

The sun is setting what a beautiful view.

I only wish is that I were sharing it with you.

My heart yearns for a day.

When we can share times like this together, if there were but a way.

To hold your hand, kiss your lips,

And watch the sailboats settle into their slips.

Tonight this will be a dream.

Tomorrow I'll remember how real it all did seem.

From My Heart and Mind

Looking across the water to where the ocean meets the sky.

The beauty of the sunset makes me question why.

Why am I here alone?

I guess the cruel fates enjoy hearing my heart moan.

Soon I'll see the stars twinkle which reminds me of your eyes.

I here your laughter on the wind as the breezes sigh.

In your arms is home to me.

Wherever it is that you may be.

Instead I am here in "paradise"...not hardly.

From My Heart and Mind

Paint on a smile.

Make them laugh all the while.

Hide the tears so they don't see.

The sorrow that lives inside of thee.

Your love for one runs very deep.

A secret you may need to forever keep.

It's not worth the risk to lose a friend.

Better to be a sad little clown to the end.

From My Heart and Mind

There is a rainbow in the sky.

I cannot reach it no matter how I try.

But it touches my heart even though it's so far away.

With hope and the promise of better times to come, no matter where I stray.

A continuing story or a new beginning

Either way I feel like I'm winning.

Tomorrow perhaps the grey clouds will part.

Or maybe the rain shall flood my heart.

If so, I'll let a smile be my umbrella and pray that I drown.

Because life is no circus for a sad, sad clown.

From My Heart and Mind

Do you understand the turmoil in my life?

The divorce was only part of my strife.

I have a girlfriend, because I needed to.

I have to tell her, "I love you, but I'm not in love with you.

I am, however, madly in love with someone from my past.

A love so big that upon eternity its shadow is cast.

Some might say this is over the top and I exaggerate.

But I know how I feel, therefore, end of debate.

From My Heart and Mind

Do you think of me and smile?

How am I, do you wonder once in a while?

Have you ever wondered if I think of you?

It would be hard for me not to.

I'd have given you the moon, had it been mine to gift.

I'll never understand what caused the rift.

You went away and left me blue.

Now like the phoenix, from the ashes, I will arise anew!

From My Heart and Mind

Alas, how long must I wait to see the moon light caress your face?

The stars sparkling in your eyes, surely will make my heart race.

To finally know the feel of your hand in mine.

To share laughter over a glass of wine.

The smell of your hair, the sweetness of your kiss.

Oh, when we are apart these things I will miss.

For now, I long to know these things of you.

Until then, being with you in a dream will have to do.

From My Heart and Mind

What do you say to someone special?

They're going through a hard time, I'd be kind and gentle.

Does she know I wouldn't hurt her?

Or is she afraid that underneath I wear a wolf's fur?

From deep inside her, I can feel her tears.

I wish that I could remove her fears.

To make her smile inside and out.

To put love back in her heart is what I'm about.

Nothing to hide and nothing fake.

Just someone to love and share life's give and take.

From My Heart and Mind

I mounted my horse and rode away.
You offered nothing to get me to stay.
Not a hug, nor kiss, nor words of love.
I rode away as the stars shown above.
I'm not a gunslinger out of the west.
Perhaps I'm just a drifter seeking rest.
You may never understand why I rode out of town
But my heart didn't find love enough to settle down.
Without the lady my heart calls home.
I am doomed to forever roam.
Like the cowboys of old, it's just me and my horse.
My life flows on like a rivers course.
As I ride, my mind calls out her name.
Alas, this vast prairie all looks the same
Empty, like my heart without Angie.
With her, I would grow roots like a tree.
Never more to feel the need to ride.
I'd give it all up to be by her side!
To be the man she wants and needs
To grow old together from love's planted seeds.
But without I'll just ride along
Just me, my horse and a sad country song.

From My Heart and Mind

Standing in the rain.

Hoping to ease the pain.

Without you by my side.

My tears the rain will hide.

Why did you go?

Why do I still love you so?

Hard to believe it's been a year.

Since I whispered in your ear.

Never again will I utter those words that ripped us apart.

When you left you took my heart.

Wish you had killed me.

So I wouldn't need to endure this agony.

I need you to come back.

To give my rainbows color instead of them being black.

So I can feel my heart beat in my chest.

Before they lay me to rest.

From My Heart and Mind

I set my mind to wonder free.

Knowing in the morning it would return with an unlocked memory.

No sound with this memory just a silent video, I know it to be,

A memory not from the past but from the future you see.

Sitting in a diner I do not know.

I came when called without question or reason to go.

just a couple in a booth two cups of coffee on the table.

A woman I try to identify but am not able.

It won't show clear the one that reached out in the night.

Now I am here and it feels right.

I replay the scene over and over again.

I don't know where or when.

This lady no doubt is special to my heart.

In her time of need I will do my part.

I know a little from what i did see.

you called, because you knew I'd come, out of my love for thee.

From My Heart and Mind

Let's see where my mind is wandering today
My thoughts are scattered every which way.
Make you laugh or just smile
Makes me feel good for a while .
I searched for beauty far and wide.
It takes a while because beauty is on the inside
It matters not what I find
Beauty will not be found with my kind.
For I am a dreamer...
Not a schemer.
I am not trying to change who you are
I love the you I know so far.
Are you my friend
More? Less? We'll see in the end.
Welcome to my circus by the seas
Oh, beware of the flying monkeys.
Look for me near the side show tent
Barker as the barker is how the billing went.
Hope to see you there
Because I miss you and I care.
And now to close this wandering mish
So long, and thanks for all the fish.

**Flying monkeys are a reference to a character by F. Baum in The Wizard of Oz.
So Long and thanks for all the fish is a reference to a book by D. Adams,
which is a part of a group of books collectively recognized as
 The Hitchhikers Guide to the Galaxy.**

From My Heart and Mind

Have you ever loved someone so much that you find yourself constantly looking for and hoping to find a message or even an emoji from them?
Anything so that you know that they're thinking of you and there's between you no problem.
You wonder how they are and what they're doing.
And your anxiety grows when you don't hear anything.
Though you've never explained exactly how you feel, you just hope they understand and feel that way too.
And you pray that someday that feeling breaks through.
Though you've never held each other in a loving or leisurely way, you find it funny.
Because you find yourself thinking of them as a big ole snuggle bunny.
While you wouldn't want to change who they are for diamonds or gold.
Holding hands with them is how you want to grow old.
A house is just a house but anywhere with them is home.
Be it Philadelphia, Paris or Rome.
The sun, the moon and the stars seem brighter when they are around.
Perhaps someday the words you'll find to explain that when they are near, how joy abounds.

From My Heart and Mind

Is there something more that I can say?

Will you sit with me beside the bay?

We'll walk along the rocky trail.

We'll watch the boats set sail.

The sails billow full with a western breeze.

The boats skip across the bay with ease.

Their beauty and grace reminds me of you.

'tis no doubt that my feelings for you are true.

My soul has mated itself to yours, with a love so pure.

As certain as the surf kisses the shore.

"I Do" words and sentiment we may never share.

My heart and soul are already there.

On my love we would sail to the moon and back.

A love so strong and true that you cannot find a crack.

I will love you longer than forever and a day.

So tell me, is there something more that I can say?

From My Heart and Mind

I fell in love with you, even though I wasn't sure that I knew what love is.

I knew it was in vain because your heart wasn't mine, it was his.

Time has passed and I am now free to follow my heart.

Yet still, there is more than distance that keeps us apart.

My heart looks forward to the day we can meet.

When I can hold you in my arms and kiss your lips so sweet.

To feel the magic of love fill the void in my soul.

To see the world become brighter, as two broken hearts become whole.

To feel your breathe against my skin.

To feel the caring warmth grow within.

To show the world the evolution of two friends.

And announce that we are that and more, from now until time ends.

Using words as bright and colorful as a rainbow's hue.

As we look in each other's eyes and say "I love you".

From My Heart and Mind

Walking through the park hand in hand.

Meant more to me than I would expect you to understand.

We weren't on a date, nor would this lead to one.

But this simple closeness helped me more than hours of therapy could have done.

While I loved you then and I love you still,

to be completely honest with you, I always will.

We shared a closeness, a silent bond.

Yet this wasn't a promise of anything beyond.

I am broken inside where no one can see.

I'm trying from my past to break free.

Starting over and building a life of my own

writing poems helps me break out of that zone.

I write of love and romance and other things I scarcely know.

Or I write from the darkness where the light is afraid to go.

For years my emotions were all that could break loose.

But I crave companionship but I fear placing my neck in a noose.

I know ultimately I have to be me and let the chips fall where they may.

And I am in love with you, and that love shall never stray.

From My Heart and Mind

It feels strange to be so at peace inside.

I've become used to the turmoil of a swirling tide.

From somewhere in the healing process, I found a light.

From a nightmare, I slipped into a dream in the night.

I followed like a sailor to the sirens call.

Disregarding the boat's fate which may fall.

Just when I thought I could no longer survive.

A phone call reminded me of the reason to stay alive.

Like an angels voice reaching my ears from above.

Touching my heart, my mind, my soul with words of love.

Only for you, I live my life strong.

The one I have been in love with all along.

From My Heart and Mind

You are my best friend and know how much I care.

Remember, that for you, I'll always be there.

When I am hurting, it is for you that I always reach.

I dream of holding your hand, as we walk along the beach.

If the moon truly inspires dreams,

Then, you are my moon it seems.

It feels natural and right, your hand in mine.

I long to kiss you, but won't cross that line.

Hugs are the most we will share to this very day.

Try as I might, my feelings for you won't waver or go away.

You may not want to know the depths of my feelings for you.

All my sorrows, pains, and wounds, you're there to see me through.

You are the one I hold in my heart, above and before any other.

From My Heart and Mind

Dearest to my soul, even beyond my sisters and brother.

Greater together than when we are apart.

Little wonder, I believe, that you hold my heart.

My friend, you see, of what life has to offer, you are the very best.

I know that I deserve the finest and will never again settle for less.

Come what may, I will stand with you, always and forever.

You are enormously loved and I'll forsake thee never.

From My Heart and Mind

Those big brown eyes twinkling as she smiles.

Just to see them, I would crawl for miles.

Her golden locks shining in the sun.

My heart knew instantly , that she is the one.

That smile so sweet, framed by lips of wine.

Somehow, I know, I must make this angel mine.

To be encased in her arms warm embrace.

Always brings a shy smile to my face.

Without even trying, she stole my heart.

Kind, funny, beautiful, and so very smart.

My soul longs to have hers' for its wife.

My heart and mind knows, she is the one true love of my life.

From My Heart and Mind

I told you that I love you.
You said I love you too.
And I know that you care.
But my life, you don't want to share.
You say you only want to be friends.
And so we'll be until time ends.
I keep praying that someday you'll see.
That in this world, you and I are meant to be.
You tell me to find myself a girl.
I'm trying to give that a whirl.
But I can't give my heart to another, you see.
Because my heart belongs to you, eternally.
I hope your life is full of love and happiness.
You certainly deserve nothing less.
If these things seemingly can't be found.
Think of me, because my heart to you is bound.
On that day, what I know now, you will see.
Then you can look at me and say, "you belong to me."
And we'll still be friends, let it be known.
Because friendship is the soil in which our seeds for the future have been sown.
I dearly love you, my friend!
And I will long after eternity has come to an end.

From My Heart and Mind

What is the size and shape of love?

It can be as endless as the skies above.

Or it can be the size of a grain of sand.

The heart shape we use has become so bland.

Love can be of any shape, I have come to know.

Like a well cut diamond, it has many facets to show.

There is love that only to the heart it reaches.

True love, to the heart, mind and soul, like high tide on the beaches.

The former is nice, but you know it will never last.

It will fade, and be fond memories in your past.

The latter is the goal of dreams for an eternal mate.

I pray that destiny will deliver that one as my fate.

This is the one I love that makes my entire being quake.

And fills my thoughts and dreams while asleep and awake.

This is a love that morphs to every shape and size.

The type of love the poets attempt to immortalize.

From My Heart and Mind

I wanted to tell you how much I care.

But when I see your face my thoughts go God knows where.

You are my inspiration, my muse.

Yet I fear how you would handle the news.

I love you beyond what I should.

The depths and complexity are in my mind very good.

Would it give you a fright,

To know that you are my sunlight?

Smart, funny and quite beautiful to me.

You'd understand, if through my heart you could see..

Afraid you need never be.

For eternally, I shall be in love with thee!

From My Heart and Mind

I'd send a poem to your printer, so no one else could see.

The heartfelt words of what you mean to me.

How your eyes speak volumes without you uttering a sound.

How a touch from your hand makes my heart pound.

Why I can hardly wait to see your face.

And ponder if a kiss would launch my emotions into outer space.

But alas, these things are going onto the pile of broken dreams.

Because your heart has been given to someone else it seems.

I care more than you'll ever know.

But oh, what the poem on the printer would show.

From My Heart and Mind

If I asked to kiss thee, would you answer yes?

Could our lives continue freely, or would it make them a mess?

I would have you as my one and only.

Never more would either of us be lonely.

If love is enough to see us through.

We'd be as one, where now there are two.

Would you hold my hand when we are together?

Be confident, for I would leave thee never.

I shall be forever by your side.

I'll never wed, unless you are my bride.

What a wonderful life together we will miss.

Because I'll never have the courage to ask you for a kiss.

From My Heart and Mind

If I told you that I love you, would you even care.

I'd like to kiss your lips and run my fingers through your hair.

I could lose myself looking in to your big brown eyes.

Your smile melts the darkest of clouds from my skies.

Soft as rose petals I imagine your skin.

Caressing it gently would stoke the fire of passion that burns deep within.

I love thee in more ways than I can count.

I would pour my love upon thee in an infinite amount.

It would be like a bottomless glass of wine.

If you would just show me a sign.

How wonderful it would be to hear four little words from you.

The words I long to hear, I love you too.

From My Heart and Mind

In my heart, you are second to none.

True love, you are my one.

But tears cascade down my face.

Because I know that in this time and place.

There are many before me in your heart.

Yet we are better together than apart.

My wish to taste your sweet lips will happen never.

Nevertheless my love for you will go on and on and far beyond forever.

From My Heart and Mind

I am going to take a long slow walk in the rain.

And let the purifying water wash away my pain.

Alone with my thoughts.

A rejuvenating experience that can't be bought.

Perhaps I'll daydream of seeing your face.

And call your name and imagine you will hear from this place.

Wishing I could hold your hand and take this walk.

I miss your eyes and how they twinkle when you talk.

How your nose crinkles when you throw me a quick smile.

and I'd wish we could walk together for another mile.

I'm glad the rain can't wash away my feelings for you.

Alas, Absence makes the heart grow fonder, I know when it comes to you that is very, very true!

Loving you is what keeps me sane.

I am going to go take a long slow walk in the rain.

From My Heart and Mind

Every once in a while,

A thought crosses my mind and I smile.

It could be a place, a joke, a song to sing.

Or perhaps a memory, a face, or just about anything.

Funny or heartwarming the smile is still the same.

Smiling at an odd, inappropriate time doesn't mean I think it's a game.

It means my brain is multitasking.

And it has touched something without my asking.

Hearing laughter in the wind, a name, a voice,

I smile because I have no choice.

From My Heart and Mind

Standing at the rail looking out to sea.

Wondering if tonight you are thinking about me.

I wish I could share the beauty of this sight.

What words could do justice to the ocean at night.

I send a postcard from each port of call.

Saying it's nice and I'm having a ball.

Only thing I'm sure of when this ship returns to its berth.

I miss you like crazy everywhere on this earth!

From My Heart and Mind

My mind is tired and begging for sleep.

The aches and pains of my body are painful and deep.

But a long drive still lies ahead.

It will be hours before I can rest my weary head.

I am not worried about drifting off tonight.

Thoughts of blessed freedom I am keeping in sight.

From this made and allowed prison soon I shall take flight.

This nightmare will end and a dream begin.

As soon as I release the truth I hold within.

From My Heart and Mind

I was hooked.

Those eyes, I never should have looked.

How could such an innocent glance

Pierce my heart like a lance.

Her smile was warm, yet shy.

I noticed the twinkle in her eye.

Our eyes locked for less than the beat of a heart.

Gone was my resistance from the very start.

What happened next I cannot recall.

But those eyes, those eyes started it all.

From My Heart and Mind

What is it that makes us fall in love?

Is it Cupid and his arrows shot from above?

Is it a matter of the heart?

How does love start?

Does it begin with a friend?

And why does love sometimes end?

I have loved and lost.

Yet I will gladly follow love no matter the cost.

There is someone that fills my heart and mind.

I know that I would walk through fire just to hold her hand in mine.

From My Heart and Mind

When I see you, my heart skips a beat.

Hearing your voice is, for my ears, such a treat.

Do you know how much I miss you when we're apart?

It's like having a blizzard blowing through my heart.

When I look into your eyes, it's hard to stay composed.

It's like flood gates opening after being too long closed.

To what can I compare my love for you?

It's stronger than gravity, deeper than the Night sky, and will last beyond eternity, these things are all true.

You are more amazing than the grandest magical feat.

That's why, when I see you, my heart skips a beat.

From My Heart and Mind

If I offered you a seat, would you sit?

If I give you my heart would you break it?

If I look into your eyes and tell you that I love you,

Would you look into mine and say I love you too?

If I ask you to dance, would you dance?

Once I was too shy, but you are worth taking the chance.

I would be honored to sit with you anytime.

Break your heart, there couldn't be a worse crime!

I would show you and tell you "I love you " everyday.

And with you as my partner, we will dance eternity away.

From My Heart and Mind

I know you didn't intend to.

But my heart was stolen by you.

Thoughts of you fill my happiest of days.

My dreams are filled with your charming ways.

How are you doing, and what's going on.

Are two of the questions which dance in my thoughts, starting daily before the dawn.

To me you are amazing and the most wonderful person on earth.

I'd create a holiday, if I could, to celebrate the day of your birth.

I wonder how the universe contains my love for you.

So beautiful and grand in everything you do.

My soul smiles at the mention of your name.

Please don't think that my love is just a game.

Never before and never again will I feel this way.

In my life forever, is where I want you to stay.

To me, you are more beautiful than the most amazing sunset.

From My Heart and Mind

I miss you so, and my heart breaks, when out of my sight you get.

How deeply I care, is beyond what words can accurately describe.

To break your heart, there isn't enough fame or fortune for me to be bribed.

My friend, love for you is engraved upon my soul.

Forever, I am yours, I hope and pray that someday, I will be your goal.

My everything, you became when my heart was stolen by you.

My love is yours for the taking, even though, I know, you never intend to.

From My Heart and Mind

Hung a dream catcher above my bed.

To keep nightmares out of my head.

It certainly worked, not a bad dream in sight.

As thoughts of you kept me safe and warm through the night.

Sigh, if only I could find the courage to tell you how I really feel.

But just being near you, I can't believe it's real.

My mind turns to mush and my pulse races so.

I just hope that my true feelings don't show.

I'm afraid that they might scare you away.

And that would surely be my darkest day.

For without you my life would be a nightmare.

Not even a dream catcher would keep me from despair.

From My Heart and Mind

Every once in a while

Things happen that make you smile.

Talking with friends, both old and new

Times to cherish for they are precious and few.

Too often we remember the things that went wrong

But those too were just brief moments in life's song.

Bad times are dark the storytellers say

That's because of how the good times light our way.

From My Heart and Mind

He sat at the keyboard trying to write away.

Nearby, sat a glass of scotch and a cigar burning in the ashtray.

The dead line for his new book's first draft to be turned in.

He'd done most of his best writing in this old cabin.

Tonight, his keys sat untouched, the words wouldn't flow.

He stared out the window and watched the falling snow.

The woman he loved was the only thing on his mind.

He'd come here to escape distraction and had left her behind.

Every thought was consumed by a longing to see her face.

In this solitude, he realized, as he stared off into space.

Forever alone, love unrequited, his heart was as worthless as a token.

A tear rolled down his cheek, he turned and typed; the block was broken.

From My Heart and Mind

The telephone rang, the voice said mom died.

My eyes welled up and cried.

Knew this day was coming.

Still the news was numbing.

After 35 years apart dad and mom are together once more.

A future without either of you lays before.

I'll do my best to make you proud.

Thank you for the lessons and the love, even when it wasn't said out loud.

Now it's our turn to be apart.

Rest In Peace Mom, I love you with all my heart!

From My Heart and Mind

The darkness approached with the intent of over taking me.

The bright light inside of me it couldn't see.

All it saw, as did the world, was the sorrow I showed.

Blinded by its thirst for the blood in my veins, that flowed.

It rushed forward, full attack, planning on taking body and soul.

It never suspected I'd face it and stop it from reaching its goal.

Like a flash of light, brighter than lightening, and the darkness screamed.

As my thoughts of you filled me with love and my eyes beamed.

The darkness never stood a chance, and it didn't have a clue.

Defeated before it started, because of how much I am in love with you!

From My Heart and Mind

The dragon awakens and opens his eyes.

Soon he'll feel the wind as he takes to the skies.

He recalls the druids and their natural ways.

Seems he has slumbered for centuries, not mere days.

What he recalls are villages and towns,

Now mega cities everywhere abounds.

He knows this from where he lay.

A connection has been made this day.

This dragon is honestly the love inside the soul of this man.

Now divorced, alone and free to do what he can.

The connection, his love for her, truer than sand.

But pairing with her, is by her command.

For her love he would wage the most savage fight.

But he takes only what she willing gives him, no matter how slight.

Respect and love for her goes on eternally.

And this dragon would treat her so tenderly.

From My Heart and Mind

What do I do when my life goes astray.

When I feel like I just want to run away.

Instead of bolting and running myself into a dead end,

I pick up the phone and reach out to my best friend.

She has helped me time and again and always has my back.

Her wisdom and advice gets me going on the right track.

I know that I am so fortunate to have her in my life every day.

The problem is, that my feelings of love for her, won't go away.

While we love each other, like best friends often do.

She is the one that makes my broken heart feel brand new.

I feel whole whenever we are together.

She's the one I'll love, cherish and adore, forever and ever!

From My Heart and Mind

Your voice I heard.

So sweet, like the song of a bird.

My heart beat stronger in my chest.

To not say, I am in love with you, is quite a test.

This however is our way.

Though my love for you grows every day.

You may want never to hear this from my lips.

Love for you, through my body and mind rips.

I love you my sweet.

Be I in a castle or on a street.

From My Heart and Mind

While enjoying a drink and a cigar.

Relaxing and looking at the stars.

A strange fog fell obscuring my views.

There in all her glory, stood my muse.

Wearing the colors in which she looks the best.

I invited her to join me, that she might rest.

I got her a drink and we sit and chat.

I am totally smitten, no doubt of that.

There is nothing about her that I don't adore.

Her touch, her eyes, her laugh, and so much more.

I found the courage to express my feelings, heartfelt and complete.

After years of longing I finally kissed those lips so sweet.

She knew that I loved her beyond all others I've known.

The fog lifts and I'm sitting there all alone.

Was she here or was it all just a dream.

On the table, two empty glasses, lit by a moonbeam.

From My Heart and Mind

I saw a quiz that asked, who will be your last kiss?

I thought about it and my answer is this.

We don't know what is yet to come.

So what I'm about to say might sound dumb.

My next kiss, if I could choose.

Would be the sweet lips of my muse.

And every kiss thereafter would be hers alone.

Never again would strange lips touch my own.

This promise I'd keep, even should the heavens fall from above.

For my last kiss I'd choose; my muse, my friend, my one true love.

From My Heart and Mind

Though I may never feel your loving embrace.
Or ever awake in the morning and see your beautiful face.
I shall forever long for your lips to kiss.
When I'm alone, you are the one I truly miss.
I would marry thee today, if you would but have me.
But I know, your heart will never let that be.
For you, we will be just forever friends.
But I shall love you long after this life ends.
Eternity is the start of how long I will be in love with you.
And daily I pray that your heart, will someday, be in love with me too.
It isn't lust, or infatuation, or some other game.
I truly love you and wish you felt the same.
You would be cherished, loved and adored.
My love, my muse, my life's musical chord.
When I say I love you, you think it's absurd.
I often wish I knew a stronger word.
My love for you is like an iceberg in the sea.
So much more, and deeper, than you can see.
Will you marry me? Are words I'd love to say.
My heart and soul are already wed to you, be that as it may.
Forever, my best friend, you will always be.
Always, my love for you, will be a part of me.
Perhaps someday, you'll take a chance with me and discover what love can do.
Because, I am deeply, madly, crazy, passionately, wonderfully in love with you!

From My Heart and Mind

From My Heart and Mind

From My Heart and Mind

About the Author

Neil Barker was born in Jersey Shore, Pennsylvania, October 29, 1964

He attended Mansfield University of Pennsylvania.

I've enjoyed writing poems in my spare time for a few years.

I've worked many jobs over the years, and have tried writing stories, in my spare time, but found I really enjoy writing poetry.

I hope you found something amongst these that touched your heart, because they were written from mine.

From My Heart and Mind